Praise for *Honey Do to Honey Done!*

"If you've ever argued about chores, this book is for you. Cheri Flake knows all about nagging — and how to put a stop to it. Her practical, no-nonsense system helps couples make love not war."

> ~ David Woodsfellow, PhD, Clinical Psychologist
> and Founder of The Woodsfellow Institute for Couples Therapy

"An excellent guide that shows couples an engaging and fun way to take care of daily chores without nagging, arguments, and hurt feelings. Flake's ingenious "Love List" helps couples keep the household running smoothly so they can focus on enjoying each other. A useful tool for married and co-habitating partners!"

> ~ Amy Lewis Bear, LPC, Author of *From Charm to Harm:*
> *The Guide to Spotting, Naming, and Stopping Emotional Abuse in Intimate*
> *Relationships*

"Finally, a way to get tasks done for your household without nagging your partner. This short book gives you a simple system to partner with your mate to get things done - without the irritation and stonewalling. A quick read with some new ideas! Enjoy!"

> ~ Casey Truffo, Marriage and Family Therapist and Founder of The
> International Therapist Leadership Institute

"Cheri Flake has managed to take a concept that is rooted in evidence-based research and make it not only easy to understand and implement, but enjoyable to read about! Her straightforward, relatable presence shines through in every page, allowing the reader to connect with her message and understand her teaching on a more personal level. I would recommend this book to anyone wanting to work on their relationship, their communication skills and their productivity. It's far more than just a book about how to get your to-do list done!"

> ~ Rebecca Clegg, LPC, Owner of Authentic Living Psychotherapy, LLC

"*Honey Do to Honey Done* is brilliant! Cheri gives couples a realistic and practical methodology and the tools they need to navigate common and tricky daily annoyances. With those out of the way, readers feel better about themselves and can focus their time in relationships on the things that matter. A must read for those looking to make a positive impact on their spousal or significant other relationships."

~ Veronica Pomeranz, LPC, Owner of Atlanta Counseling and Wellness, LLC

"*Honey Do to Honey Done!* is truly a relationship game changer. ... Author Cheri Flake has a great system that will help you get done what needs to be done. It's easy to follow and as long as you treat it as a full system, you can have amazing results. ... I encourage anyone in a relationship to try this and especially anyone starting a long-term relationship so you get off the ground the right way. This is a great book for newlyweds and should be included at every wedding shower. Bottom line: She nailed it!"

~ A. Bernette, Interfaith Minister and Author of *Chosen, Crossed*, and *How to Write a Four Week First Draft*

"Cheri Flake's *From Honey Do to Honey Done!* accomplishes what so many marriage therapists forget – that it's the basics of life that create a marriage. This is a no-nonsense method that takes the sting out of couples' disagreements. Flake draws from solid behavioral science without becoming caught up in theoretical mumbo jumbo in a very accessible way."

~ Moshe R. Manheim, LCSW, Family and Couples Therapist

"Cheri's tools and enthusiastic coaching provide a skillful and sustainable path for creating a successful and mutually respectful homemaking partnership. This fun book opens the door to enjoying a shared life that is free from nagging's negative and corrosive consequences. A true win-win for couples!"

~ Tom Johnson, Director of Information Access - retired, The Coca-Cola Company (and married for 43 years!)

"Cheri Flake has brought her inimitable energy and enthusiasm to a commonly difficult set of issues and offers insightful, practical, do-able and fun new perspectives and behaviors to make positive changes in intimate relationships. I give this work 5 stars!"

~ Paul Olander, LCSW, JD, Director of Behavioral Health Services at DeKalb Medical Center

Honey Do to Honey DONE!

A Simple System for a Productive and Happy Household

With Absolutely No More Nagging!

by

Cheri Augustine Flake, LCSW

Printed in the United States of America

First Edition

For permission to reproduce selections from this book, please write to the publisher:

Permissions, The Stress Therapist, LLC
3104 Briarcliff Road #98297
Atlanta, GA 30359

The author of this book does not dispense medical advice or prescribe the use of any technique as a form of treatment for physical, emotional, or medical problems without the advice of a physician, either directly or indirectly. The intent of the author is to only offer information of a general nature to help you in your quest for emotional and spiritual well-being. In the event you use any of the information in this book for yourself, the author and the publisher assume no responsibility for your actions.

Book design by Pixel Studios

Cover stock photo by DepositPhotos

ISBN:
0-9979509-1-9
978-0-9979509-1-5

For information about the author, please visit www.TheStressTherapist.com

For Andrew, with boundless gratitude for all you do for me.

Contents

The Lowdown

Who wants to be nagged? Nobody. Who feels like nagging? Nobody. Furthermore, nagging almost always creates an argument and gives rise to resentment in both parties involved. Sure, arguing can sometimes be healthy, and there are undoubtedly many therapists and books addressing how to argue constructively -- but many times it is *removing the argument altogether,* including even the potential for an argument, that is the best way to go.

This book is all about working together as a couple so you can eliminate nagging for good. When the nagging is gone, so are the multitude of problems that inevitably come along with nagging. Wouldn't it be nice to kiss the "big fight" goodbye forever? And, here's the great news -- it's not only possible, but relatively simple if you follow my outline presented here in this book.

I can hear the groans already…"Awesome. So, nagging won't be the reason we fight. But I can guarantee that if I don't nag, he won't do it. So, we'll just fight about everything he said he would do and never did instead." Here again, no worries. The coolest thing about this little system that I will teach you is that it not only knocks out all of the nagging, it knocks out all of the items on the "Honey Do" list as well.

The system is called "The Love List," and it can help oil the gears of your relationship and household, getting them running like a well oiled machine. The Love List both draws on and produces more love, all the while getting the job done. The best part is that this simple little system promises all of this without any nagging whatsoever.

Things to know:

✓   By setting agreed-upon ground rules, the Love List removes the potential for arguments and nagging.

✓   The Love List gets all of the household tasks and family chores *done!*

The Inspiration

Research indicates that we have 60,000 thoughts a day. If this is truly the case, then it can be assumed that most of our thoughts are wildly repetitive. After all, if the majority of thought was creative, we would be having epiphanies all day long! So I think it is safe to assume that of those 60,000 daily thoughts, we've probably had 55,000 or 58,000 of the same thoughts, yesterday and the day before that and the day before that and so on...

A big part of my practice is teaching my clients to free up brain space and make room for creative and eventually even joyful thoughts, by minimizing how many thoughts that we have each day; namely, the thoughts that we seem to have over and over that don't do us any good and may even generate intense feelings of stress.

These thoughts may seem totally benign but can truly begin to affect our lives in a miserable way. Thoughts that seem normal and even neutral to us have the potential, when we start to repeat them, to make us feel horrible and paralyze us. Thus, a seemingly neutral thought like, "I need to get my house organized and decluttered," will connect with a more highly charged, previously held belief like, "People with messy houses are lazy." What results is a new, negative attribute that we logically then must believe to be true; that is, "I'm a lazy person."

Repetition only reinforces the new negative. Therefore, repetitive thoughts like, "I wish I had a garden. Why won't I just start one?" or, "I just can't decide where to put it, but I really want fresh vegetables," or, "My cooking would be so much better if I grew my own veggies," may become, "Maybe I *do* have a problem with commitment if I can't even pick a space to start a garden," or, "I guess I'm not the type of person who grows fresh vegetables," or, "I say I'm going to have my own garden but I'm full of it." These thoughts may eventually twist into, "I never do what I say I'm going to do," "I'm a fraud," or, "I'm just a big jerk." Thoughts that may have seemed pretty insignificant have now changed into pretty horrible thoughts. We know from cognitive psychology that these thoughts are harmful because of the principle that if we think a thought enough, we will begin to believe it whether it's true or not. So, through repetition we start to credit all of these untrue thoughts, forming beliefs that merit that the self-description that they validate is actually *true*!

The bottom line is this: Repetitive thoughts that have to do with mundane tasks have the potential to become huge stressors when they have been on "the to-do list" for far too long. This metamorphosis makes us feel pretty bad, and in turn, because our brains avoid things that we feel bad about, we perpetuate putting things off again and again. It is a classic vicious cycle.

Soon enough, it becomes easy to think of ourselves as hopeless procrastinators or wonder if we're grappling with an attention problem if we can't get the job done at home or in our personal life. Sadly, the failure to get our act together at home gives credibility to the multitude of thoughts becoming beliefs that make us feel awful, thereby squelching our motivation and keeping our desires a far cry from reality.

Furthermore, since your brain wants nothing more than to be right, it starts to take on even more of the characteristics of "the procrastinator" to validate your untrue beliefs. This adaptation makes the situation even worse! Now, we're able to see "proof" in our lives that we're stuck and experience the uncomfortable thought that we might be stuck for good. In no time at all, our brains our telling us that we are innately lazy, a perpetual procrastinator, or just a bad spouse, parent or person.

The saddest part of all is that we start feeling really horrible about things that we actually *do* want in our lives, in our homes and with our families. Since we have chosen to share our lives with someone else, we inevitably bring them into the picture. When our egos just can't take it anymore, and in an effort to protect ourselves, we may resort to shooting these ugly thoughts and attributes toward our partner. "I would paint the garage if he would organize all those tools. He's so lazy!" Or, "How am I supposed to get organized in the basement with all of her crap in the way? She's so messy!" Or, "Why should I do all of this by myself, it's his house, too! He should care more!" Ugly thoughts bring ugly feelings and behaviors along with them and leave the

13

door wide open for complaints, arguing and nagging. All of these negative thoughts build up and the resulting vast resistance on everyone's part means that both spouses are fundamentally ignoring what is really going on.

What is really going on is this: You chose each other. Presumably, you love each other. Furthermore, in a marriage or long-term partnership it is safe to assume that no one is going anywhere. It behooves both of you to make a change now, in your commitment and in your communication patterns to make your life together better. Arguing about light bulbs or cutting the grass is not "what it's all about." You probably won't be lying on your deathbed thinking, "I really wish I would have finished that last load of laundry," or, "I bet he just drove over here and didn't make our bed before he left the house," or, "I bet she forgot to put the alarm on again today. We're probably getting robbed as we speak!" No. So, let's get back to what makes you happy and what brings you joy.

It's safe to assume that when you chose your partner in life, you saw the potential this person and this new relationship had to bring you happiness. And hopefully, you continue to experience happiness in your relationship for much of the time. So why not eliminate the other parts altogether and focus on increasing this happiness? What most of us tend to forget is there is an abundance of joy in the present moment. Let us please stop arguing about what needs to be done in the future and instead live a little in the Now. Because truly, as Dr. Wayne Dyer wisely observed, "We are not human *do*ings, we are human *be*ings."

When you can just *be* with your partner, that is, spend time together that is not "productive" in the traditional sense, but productive in the cultivation of your relationship and love for one another...well, then life together is kinder and much, much grander.

In order to be a little bit better, that is a little bit happier in our everyday living, we need to free up some of our cluttered, repetitive and uninspired thinking. This need exists for both the couple and the individual level. Sometimes starting with the daily hassles can be the first step in de-cluttering *all* parts of your life.

One of the simplest ways that we can free up our thought space is by stopping any discussions with our partners that tend to result in a fight or disagreement. Typically, avoiding hot topics causes tension to intensify, but the method I am about to teach you allows you to get the job done, fully develop your ideas, answer your questions and resolve your issues with minimal *verbal* discussion and ideally, no nagging whatsoever.

The key is that we eliminate the potential for these repetitive task-oriented thoughts to become nasty by making sure that they have no place to live and therefore cannot continue to hound us in our mind. When our brain knows that a task has been addressed as part of a system that works, the buzz of repetitive thoughts can subside. This in turn diminishes the time and energy drain on the relationship of a constant focus on, and drawn-out conversations about, the mundane. We replace recurring daily hassles and worry thoughts with a plan and system. Now, you have room for new, creative thought. Of course, all of this also means no more nagging!

Once you have a plan and system in place that you are consistently using, the power of habit comes into play. Habit is huge for the Love List and its long-term success. Think of it this way, nobody gets in the shower and contemplates what to do in there…we just come out clean. Over the years of repetitive showering it has all become automatic, thereby freeing up thought space for creativity and maybe even a song. What if you could apply this shower mentality to a household task? Or many? The Love List aims to make your household chores (and your partner's chores!) simply normal; that is, something you automatically do without stress, procrastination or excuses. Also, the big bonus is that we are using a tool that uses, spreads and feeds on love. Habitual love sounds pretty good, doesn't it?

A lot of day-to-day tasks are pretty boring or unpleasant to complete or discuss but because they need consistent care, they become a permanent topic of conversation giving rise to arguing, animosity, frustration or endless talking about chores. Some items are never addressed and the importance of them fades away in the background as the more pressing issues demand our day-to-day attention. Ignoring some items may seem like the easier route, but it hurt us in the end. You can put off the talk about getting together a will or even a retirement plan without any immediate repercussions, but if you don't take out the garbage, pay the bills, or fix the toilet, life is going to be stressful and hard. Fueled again and again with negativity, boring tasks become miserable tasks.

Habit can change everything. When miserable tasks become

habitual, they revert back to being boring tasks. When boring tasks become habitual, time -- often seen as our greatest commodity -- opens up, creative thought moves in, and all of the sudden these tasks don't seem so boring anymore. When boring tasks become just regular day-to-day tasks that are being completed regularly and aren't constantly causing discord, they don't harbor any negativity anymore. It all becomes about as eventful as a shower.

I will show you how to get all of these tasks done, moving from the typical situation to the luxury of time freed up to talk about your beautiful angels (or holy terrors, depending on the day), what's on your mind, how your day went or how you'd like it to go, what brings you together or just good old fashioned make-out sessions. Men hate to be nagged and frankly, women hate nagging. It just seems necessary sometimes to get what you want, right? No more!

Imagine spending quality time with your partner again, much like you did when you were dating. No more conversations about household duties like cleaning the litter box, pressure washing the deck or paying the gas bill. Imagine these items already checked off of the list or already having a coveted spot on the calendar *with* a plan! This means that you get to spend your time together catching up, making decisions about that vacation, or just laughing or being romantic.

Isn't this what you signed up for anyway?

It seems too good to be true, I know. But over the years, I have taught many couples this simple system with great success. I am also walking the walk; I use this system in my own household as well.

Things to Know:

- ✓ We have about 60,000 thoughts a day! Freeing up the mundane, task-oriented thoughts can provide space for peaceful, creative and even joyful thoughts.

- ✓ We begin to believe thoughts that we have over and over whether they are true or not!

- ✓ Repetitive, useless thoughts about what needs to be done in our lives can actually cause us harm if we do not address them.

- ✓ When a partnership is struggling to keep up with household and familial tasks, we feel bad about the relationship and in come nagging and criticism.

- ✓ According to our brains, things that we feel bad about are to be avoided at all costs. Thus, the potential for procrastination is created.

- ✓ Over time, the Love List uses the power of habit and thus, frees up time and makes space for creative thought.

- ✓ A system that eliminates negative thoughts and beliefs regarding the household and gets the couple working as a team, makes the relationship stronger. Life is more fun and all parties are happier.

The Goal

"No more nagging" to wives means we don't feel like super crabapples anymore. We also don't feel alone in our household endeavors. We learn that we can actually count on our man! Let's face it, women are mostly running their households whether they are also working outside the home or not. The research backs up this observation: The buck stops with the woman of the house when it comes to keeping it all up. Some of the biggest arguments my female clients have are over assumptions about who is responsible for specific housework or other domestic duties, a general lack of appreciation when the work is executed well, or feelings of loneliness or decision-making fatigue. Feeling like you are working as a team is a game changer for women. It's not all you anymore!

"No more nagging" to husbands means no more complaints or criticism. And, here's the kicker, ladies: What you consider to be criticism is much different than what your man considers to be criticism (I'll get to this soon). Rather than trying to figure it all out from his perspective, why not totally eliminate what could be construed as criticism? That is, make all nagging go away. Forever.

I realize that I am assuming the wife is on the giving and the husband on the receiving end of nagging. The roles are actually more fluid, and I will be getting into the particulars and exceptions later. For now, know that for *any* couple, regardless of roles, gender or other details, the time they save *not* reviewing what needs to be done, what they are disappointed about, or who committed to do what, is newly freed up *quality* time with each other. I mean *real* quality, free of resentment, sensitive or touchy "land mine" subjects, or silently harbored grievances.

The Love List system not only ends all nagging, it actually gets whatever she's been crabbing about, and he's been complaining about, *done*. It works so amazingly well that I can't help but want to share it with as many people as possible. This method is a breeze to initiate and sustain and is a resilient enough marital tool that you can use it forever.

Because my system keeps both parties held responsible and in check, this method has been a true life-changer in many of my clients' marriages as well as in my own. There is no more room for occasional whining or defiance because, in a spirit of mutual respect, the couple has agreed upon and worked out how they will follow through on what needs to be done. The ground rules are clear. And don't worry, there is a place for grievances and problems that may arise, but it is all done in kindness and with love.

This is why I call this method "The Love List." I am delighted to share with you just how it works and how it can change everything for the better in a simple and easy-to-implement way.

Things to Know:

✓ The goal when using the Love List is for the couple to regain or even enhance the best aspects of their relationship prior to all of the responsibilities that come from running a household and family together.

✓ Not only does the couple's relationship benefit from the Love List, but the household tasks and items are actually *done,* making all parties involved happier.

The Usual

The Love List was created to cater to the individual differences that make up a couple. Now, there are exceptions to every rule and having taught the Love List to hundreds of people, I have encountered virtually all of them. I have worked with couples who fit traditional gender roles, that is, where the male works full time and the female stays at home. I have worked with couples who have children and couples who do not. I have taught this method to working moms, stay-at-home moms, working dads and stay at home dads. I have taught the Love List to *many* same-sex couples, both men and women. I feel confident in stating that the system works regardless of the circumstances of your particular coupledom. In consideration for the range of diversity in couples as well as applying what has worked for my clients, I will be working with a sample couple who will have the characteristics of what is *usually* true. That is, we will be going the traditional route for simplicity and if your partnership differs from this "norm," you can simply pick who each of you would be in the following scenario and go from there. With that, meet our "typical" couple: Joey and Susie.

Joey is a dad and works full time. Susie is a mom and works part time. They have been married for ten years and they have two young children in elementary school.

Susie takes on the bulk of the household and childcare responsibilities. In general, she is OK with this as she works less outside of the home, but needs help from Joey that often feels difficult to obtain. When Susie feels overwhelmed with household obligations, she resorts to nagging Joey to get things done around the house. She has made many "Honey Do" lists that are sometimes honored and sometimes ignored. This makes Susie think Joey is unreliable and this only adds to her stress level. She feels resentful when Joey caters to his hobbies or goes out with his friends because she doesn't feel like she has any free time at all. She nags, but this never motivates Joey and nagging only seems to make things worse.

Joey enjoys his job, but it can be stressful at times. He appreciates all that his wife does around the house and with the kids but he may not mention or show his appreciation as much as Susie might like. He really looks forward to coming home from work and being with his family, but sometimes, because Susie lacks any other time or way to raise with Joey what needs to be done, Joey feels bombarded with complaints and nagging as soon as he walks through the door. Joey is often confused as to why Susie is so upset. He doesn't think she understands how hard he is working for the whole family. He may then feel like a hard day's work was for nothing. He feels like most of their conversations revolve around what he is doing wrong. In general, he then starts to withdraw when Susie is "in a mood." Joey feels micromanaged and criticized and he wants the nagging to stop.

Things to Know:

✓ The Love List can work for you no matter the details of your particular coupledom. As you read, identify who is the "Joey" and who is the "Susie" in your relationship based not on sex or gender, but on your existing communication patterns.

The Difference

The whole point of the Love List is to eliminate verbal communication regarding household items altogether. As awesome as this is, it does not account for the communication issues that the two of you may be experiencing regarding other items that absolutely need to be discussed or that can arise in even casual conversations about your day. Because you've decided to spend a lifetime together, it behooves the both of you to pick up a little general knowledge about gender differences in communication. Not only will these vignettes about Joey and Susie validate that you do indeed need a new system that works for both of you, but this section will also provide insights about your partner that may have eluded you thus far. I will also introduce a few tools for both of you to try the next time a miscommunication or disagreement comes up.

Now, let us go over a few typical gender differences in communication that Joey and Susie are probably grappling with on a day-to-day basis. With respect to communication patterns, in general, when stressed or needing to make a decision, Joey tends to want to *think* things over and Susie tends to want to *talk* things over. Again, there are exceptions to every rule, but this is generally true. These tendencies make resolution difficult as Susie may move toward Joey to resolve or discuss an issue whereas Joey may need to pull back a bit first. Joey may then feel like he is under attack, while Susie will feel unheard.

Not surprisingly then, the number one complaint about their spouses from married women like Susie is that they don't feel listened to or heard by their partners. When Susie goes to Joey to ask him to do something or help her with something, and Joey responds by being defensive or dismissive, Susie's feelings are hurt and she doesn't feel like Joey even heard her side. When Joey then does nothing to take care of items that she has expressed are important to her regarding household and childcare responsibilities, the inaction validates her hurt feelings. Susie feels more isolated, more misunderstood and more alone in what she believes are household and parenting endeavors. These feelings quickly turn into resentment, leading Susie to resort to nagging. She thinks that quick digs are her only way to motivate her husband to listen, help or get engaged in any way.

On the other hand, the most frequent complaint from married men like Joey is that they often feel criticized by their spouse. Furthermore, Joey is likely to associate all nagging with criticism. That is, nagging to Joey is an indication that he is doing or did something wrong, or that his competence is being questioned. He feels as though Susie is not supportive of him in the relationship. As a result, Joey shuts down and sometimes stops communicating altogether, thinking that since anything he says is wrong and is met with criticism, he might as well say nothing at all.

When I am working with Susie, it often comes to a surprise to her that Joey is likely to consider *any* complaint -- *even if the complaint has absolutely nothing to do with Joey or their relationship* -- as criticism. Why? According to the prevalent Western cultural view, which was likely part of Joey's upbringing, his job as a husband is to make his wife happy. If she isn't, for whatever reason, he must have failed in his spousal duties. This belief may be conscious or unconscious, but it kicks in when he hears his wife complain or express any negative feelings at all. After all, a good husband protects his wife from feeling bad. Furthermore, Joey's friends or colleagues have probably never come to him with a problem unless they wanted him to solve it. It's unlikely that Joey has any experience with just talking things over and in his mind, frankly, this seems pointless. Something else that may be coming into play is that when Joey was little, he was probably reprimanded at some point for sharing feelings or crying and told to work it out and "be a man." Joey's mantra is "resolve it and move on."

This conditioning, incidentally, explains the age-old "Why won't he just stop and ask for directions?" argument. For Joey, brought up to prize independence and self-sufficiency, asking for help in the form of directions risks looking weak. Thank goodness for GPS!

Because of his mode of thinking, when I'm working with Joey, one of things he often finds unbelievable is that when Susie comes to him with a problem, she is *almost always not looking for a solution to her problem.* Rather, she is looking for Joey to validate that there *is* a problem and to let her share how she has handled it thus far. Susie has been brought up to always talk over how she feels and "Let it all out." Her friends have always allowed for this and she is also an expert on the flip side, having provided this comfort and understanding for her friends as well. Since Susie has had a lifetime of success in solving problems using the art of conversation, when Joey quickly jumps from discussing the problem to suggesting ideas for resolution, Susie becomes confused and hurt.

A typical encounter along these lines plays out when Susie has had a bad day. Since Susie tends to feel better after talking things through with someone, she will often seek out Joey because she loves him the most. Joey's most natural response is to instantly move into the role of the hammer; that is, seeing everything as a nail and, by hammering every single thing that Susie mentions, trying to "fix" items as quickly as possible. His heart is in the right place. Joey's hammer behavior is an effort to reassure Susie that everything is ok and he is able to handle whatever she brings him. A man of the house indeed! Although he may *try* to listen, the temptation to act assertively is overwhelming!

However, when Joey immediately "hammers" by suggesting fixes, or when that does not work, withdraws out of helplessness, Susie barely feels heard. She can't understand why he looks fidgety and uncomfortable as if he must perform or come up with the pivotal answer that will solve everything. The kicker is, if Joey could just listen quietly for a bit, respond with validating nods, eye contact and even and occasional, "I get what you mean," and leave it at that, Susie actually *will* begin to feel better and walk away feeling validated and less anxious.

If Joey tries to restrain himself from "hammering" right away, he may still become fidgety, shifting his eyes and expressing comments that are meant to validate, like "Sure" and "Uh huh," in an unintentionally curt way. Susie can't stand either one of these responses because after all, her friends would never! She may become sidetracked and lose sight of the original problem. She will first try to guide Joey into a role that for him is very uncomfortable. She may stop and address Joey's resistance with, "Can't you just listen?" or, "Yes, I could try that but do you understand why I feel like this?"

But when she raises these concerns that seem directed at him, Joey feels hopeless regarding his role to help her feel better. Joey might just shut down knowing that he's had little success in "doing the right thing" in these situations. This infuriates Susie, because instead of focusing on her concerns, Joey has become defensive and takes on an attitude like, "What do you expect *me* to do?!" To her, this shift in focus away from her problem comes across as selfish and mean. Joey, in turn, becomes even more irate because, after all, he was just trying to help her come up with a good solution to her problem and suddenly, he's the jerk.

Or, when Joey still can't or won't shift gears to engage in more listening and less "hammering," Susie's disappointment or suggestion that he is not listening reinforces his original assumptions. This conversation must be about some complaint directed at him or some supposed personal flaw. This further validates his belief that regardless of what is going on with Susie, if she's not happy, it's his fault. And indeed, at this point Susie moves on from wanting to share the original problem to now *actively* criticizing Joey by telling him that he is not acting the way she wishes that he would. Ironically, at this point the issue actually *is* more about Joey's inadequacies rather than Susie's problem!

When Joey then says that he feels attacked and starts saying things like, "I don't know what you want me to do!" and Susie responds with, "I don't want you to *do* anything, I just want you to listen to me!" everybody loses. The attention is on Joey's "wrong" behavior, not on Susie's problem. Susie is most certainly *not* getting heard and Joey most certainly *is* being criticized. Both Susie and Joey emerge from this encounter confused, hurt and frustrated.

The problems here lie on both sides. Let's start with Susie. For her part, Susie is not crediting Joey's inherent need to offer solutions regarding her bad day. Even though Susie may simply want to process an issue right away, she will need to remember Joey's need to reflect and consider. Susie will need to be patient and resist the compulsion to try to get Joey to discuss things before he is ready. She may perhaps need to find someone else to talk things over with while she gives Joey time to think things over. She may bring up an issue and say, "Can you give that some thought?" and then *walk away*. Susie will know when Joey is ready to talk when he casually mentions it to her or she asks, "Did you get a chance to think that over?" and Joey says, "Yes."

For his part, Joey cannot resist the temptation to move the conversation toward resolution and everything escalates. Joey will need to use patience when listening to Susie entirely, ask for clarification occasionally, and allow her to totally spill until she feels better. Joey will need to resist the compulsion to solve the problem for her before Susie is ready. Joey will know that Susie wants his opinion when she asks for his opinion.

When both sides follow these guidelines, they can improve communication by leaps and bounds. The result is so sudden it can seem magical. I remember one incident when my husband Andrew and I had pretty much decided that we were moving. This is quite a big deal for a family. I began asking some hard questions and Andrew naturally wanted to think it over. Honoring this, I began walking away. Then, he called me back and said, "Don't mention this to anyone for now." He wanted to keep the matter between us and not, by casually announcing something we had not fully considered ourselves first, bring in other people's opinions too early. I told him right away that this wasn't fair. After all, he was going to have the opportunity to think things over and I was getting cheated out of my desire to talk things over. I'll never forget the resulting moment of recognition. He looked up, obviously considering this point, and said, "You're right. That won't work for you." After a beat or two he then suggested that I talk it over with my best friend, but *only* my best friend, and ask her to keep it to herself for now. We both got to deal and process in our most natural and comfortable ways and all was well and wonderful with us!

When practicing this new and conscientious way of communicating, I often tell my Susies to try a little humor. Go ahead and tell Joey when exactly you need a girlfriend and proceed with a fun declaration that can be super engaging and quite loving. When Susie truly feels like she would benefit from a communicator of her own sort, she can approach Joey with a simple, "I need you to step out of hammer mode and well, just be a girl for me right now. Listen. Act how you think my girlfriend would act just for a few minutes." Pause for Joey to make a shift and acknowledge this, and then say, "Look at this shower curtain! Isn't it gorgeous! I got it on sale!" This can actually end up being really funny. The kicker is, Susie actually feels wonderful when Joey contemplates the shower curtain and nods in agreement and Joey actually feels needed and helpful on the way out of the bathroom.

Another way to practice these new communication skills in a humorous way is to "file a complaint." This works especially well at my house, I suspect, because my husband is a lawyer. If Susie has a complaint, *that doesn't have anything to do with Joey* and isn't relying on any answers, she simply says, "I would like to file a complaint." She pauses for his attention and proceeds, "The dog won't stop grabbing my shoes and hiding them all over the house! I think she's hoarding them to chew on them later or something… it's driving me nuts!" This practice really drives home the idea of offering up a concern and not needing the solution that Joey craves nor the extended conversation that Susie craves. Filing a complaint also takes the focus off of the couple and on to daily hassles that feel less important and even occasionally humorous. But the best part about filing a complaint is that it teaches Joey that, even if everything isn't perfect with Susie, it's not personal, it's just business.

In short, when a couple fails to appreciate and adapt to gender differences, this failure can make for communication disasters. Susie feels bad because she doesn't feel heard or understood by Joey. Joey feels bad because he thought Susie needed him to help in some way and what he tries obviously never works. Both communication patterns perpetuate an unworkable situation that worsens as the days, weeks and years go by. Because nagging perpetuates this poor communication pattern, the process becomes self-fulfilling: Joey *is* being criticized now, and Susie is *not* being heard.

Luckily, I have a lovely solution for both Joey and Susie!

Things to Know:

✓ Problem-solving modes and stress-coping mechanisms differ by role: Joey tends to want to *think* things over, and Susie tends to want to *talk* things over.

✓ Joey's biggest complaint is probably that he often feels criticized. Susie's biggest complaint is probably that she often feels unheard.

✓ Trying out new ways of talking to each other that honor gender differences in communication can be a great way to engage lovingly and get everyone's needs met in a lighthearted way.

✓ Even communication patterns that are perfectly normal

for each spouse over time can become quite detrimental, because they continually misalign the couple.

The Pre-Game

Chances are that in the past, Susie has attempted to put together numerous "To Do" lists for Joey. Sometimes, Joey completes every item on the list, sometimes he ignores the list, and sometimes he completes some items and neglects the rest. The lack of consistency is frustrating. Sometimes, there is no list at all but just a discussion, then a reminder, then another (now entering nagging territory) and another. Sometimes, Joey and Susie argue about various items on the list. With no consistency in either when lists are generated or due, or when items get completed, the topic of open items surfaces at the most inopportune times. The mere thought of, say, mowing the lawn, then becomes either infuriating or the subject of dread, and something to be avoided at all costs. This cycle triggers conflict and further perpetuates the problem.

When things *do* get done, Joey is not likely to get praised for his work. Susie, who does her work without nudging or praise, may be resistant to praising; that is, she may feel that this is just the way of the world. However, if Susie can get past this and actually give praise and recognition for a job well done, she will learn quite quickly that *her* life actually gets better and happier in the long run. Furthermore, Joey learns that the more he's on top of things at home, the more his wife tells him how great he is. The result is that everyone wins: Susie feels heard and Joey feels appreciated.

Before we discuss how to break this cycle for good, let me share a few suggestions that will help you get the most out of this book.

First, it may seem that the majority of my advice relies on Susie being open and often initiating change. It may not seem fair for Susie to take on the bulk of the responsibility first and upfront. However, Susie is usually the most unhappy and therefore more open to leading the way to a positive and lasting change. Simply put, if you are the one who is unhappy because of someone else's behavior, *you* are the one with the problem, not the other person. Sad but true. The good news is that it is not true that people don't change. You get people to change by changing yourself and your behaviors. In the end, Joey will absolutely have to put some effort in, but yes, the jumpstart may fall on Susie for now. Furthermore, the changes that I'm suggesting for Susie are relatively simple. A new attitude, a statement or two and a couple of tasks later and voila! Susie gets exactly what she wants. A small price to pay, indeed.

Next, *it is imperative that you follow these instructions verbatim*, because I do know this: If the two of you don't get it together and working right the first time, the likelihood that you will try again is very, very low. Taking the time on the front end will pay off, I promise.

The importance of following a proven method from the get-go and throughout makes me think of a time in which my ability to do just that got me the payback of a lifetime. A few years ago, my husband and I were in New Orleans with my baby and my almost 2-year-old. We overheard two couples discussing potty training and, intrigued because we were struggling with this upcoming transition ourselves, we began eavesdropping. It seems that one couple had read a particular book[1] whose methods yielded magical results. As we heard the explanation, my husband and I certainly wanted to get our hands on a copy of this book! After all, our son was approaching this milestone and what did we know about potty training?

We were eventually forced to admit that we were listening to their conversation when we asked for the name and the author of the book. The couple became even more animated, singing the praises of the method, the author and the quick results that they got. They explained that the author had many biological children, as well as a couple that she had adopted, and that she had trained them all herself. They positively lit up telling me that the book covered what to tell teachers or other family members to do during the process and even had a chapter on dealing with multiples. Clearly, this author was the real deal and an expert in the field.

"Really?" I said as I too began to get excited about a quick method for my boy, "Totally potty trained? Even at night?"

---

1   Jensen, Lora. *3 Day Potty Training: Start Friday, Done Sunday!* 3rd Edition. 2001. www.3daypottytraining.com

"Well…" the wife of one couple paused, "We didn't do what she suggested for night training, so no, our daughter still wears pull-ups at night. The author says this confuses them, but who can expect your kid to be dry overnight at only two years old?"

I didn't get it. Didn't they just tell me how much expertise the author had? Furthermore, I did think it would confuse a toddler to be allowed to wet her pants at night, but stay dry all day. I vowed then that once we got our hands on the book, we would follow it to the letter. After all, what if it worked?

When we returned home, my husband and I read the book and strictly followed the author's recommendations. We even went along with pointers that we were sure wouldn't work with our kid. And guess what? It worked perfectly. In fact, as I write this, my children are five and six years old and neither one has wet their pants OR their bed in YEARS.

My point is this: A system is, by nature, integrated and interdependent. If you only adopt parts of a system, only parts of your life might get better or the system may not work at all. So, why not just take the plunge and commit to this system in its entirety, not just a few components of it, but to the whole shebang?

I can assure you that the Love List has worked with my clients and even with my family over and over again. Make the commitment now. I'm just saying: What if it works?? (And, if anyone asks, I want that on my tombstone).

You just can't say that it doesn't work, if you don't try it first.

As we embark on this journey together, I wish you a mere three days of focused potty training and a lifetime of dry underpants and sheets.

Now, let's do this!

Things to Know:

✓   Regardless of how it has gone down in the past, it's time to let it go. People change when you change.

✓   For optimal results, it is imperative that you follow the Love List system verbatim. If you go into it half-heartedly and it flops, you may blame the system and never try it out again.

Things to Do:

✓   Susie, it's time to try something different! Begin praising Joey for tasks completed *even if he has never praised you for the same task*. As infuriating as this may be to even consider, know that Joey will change a bit when you change a bit and here is your big chance to prove that and actually start getting what you want…It's easier than you think and super worth it, I promise!

The Setup

You may be surprised to learn that in my therapy practice, I do not work with couples. In fact, I have only ever worked with individuals and I absolutely love this approach and practice. It is very satisfying to have your client run home with ideas and tools for change and watch them grow in their partnership without my ever having seen their spouse. Over the years, I have become pretty adept at teaching Joeys and Susies how to bring up the Love List, implement it into their relationship and home and keep it going for the long haul. Even though the Love List benefits all in the end and can be pretty exciting at first, how it is initiated and integrated into the household is very important and worth addressing before you steamroll your partner with an enthusiasm that may, without careful consideration, just lead to more disappointment and dead ends.

The best part about the Love List is that you implement it as a team. So, when bringing up the Love List initially, no matter whose idea it is, you must approach it as a project you will approve together and implement together and as to which you both have equal input. You must absolutely avoid making the Love List just more ammunition for nagging, e.g., "We have to do this, I don't know what else to do with you!" or "I can't take it anymore, do you have any better ideas?" Attempting to guilt a partner into adopting it or otherwise forcing the system will only generate resistance, and this book will end up in the sad company of other unrealized good intentions.

Since we know that there is an issue in your relationship and household that you would like to improve, we'll start there, but with a bit of a twist. Both of you have goals that are different and that the Love List can resolve, but presumably, only one of you is reading these words. To get Joey or Susie to agree to the Love List, then, you will have to actually see their side of the story. Isn't it amazing?! You haven't even started and already the Love List has you seeing *their* side!

This insight relies on the "Love" part of the system. The reason that you must see both the problem *and* the resolution from your *spouse's* perspective, is so you can articulate well what your spouse will get from using the Love List, and therefore inspire him or her to agree to try it. For now, and just to get everyone on board, you must resolve to appeal to what your *spouse wants*, not what *you* want.

Susie, remember Joey's need for reflection. You cannot start talking with Joey about the Love List in the same way you would with your girlfriend and expect an immediate and enthusiastic commitment. It just won't work. I get that you and your bestie could resolve world peace over a latte and an hour-long chat, but

Joey will need more time (and much of it without you) to think things over on his own.

Joey, you will need to sit with some of these ideas for a while yourself, and then when you are ready to talk with Susie, you'll need to keep her needs in mind. Once you bring up the Love List, you will need to be prepared for a full-on discussion and perhaps, even a barrage of questions. You will not get Susie's sign off on a new anti-nagging system if you are (a) using the word "system" too frequently or (b) using the word "nag" as anything other than a verb. Susie will check out, walk out, or flip out.

Instead, let's look at what *will* work in getting your significant other to be interested in the Love List and then agreeing to give it a try.

Susie, you need to let Joey know that a change is on the horizon. Mention that there is a system out there that stops all nagging and lets the couple check off tasks as "done" -- with virtually no verbal communication. This latter point is usually the hot ticket. "Hey, I read this book about a household system that ends all nagging! What do you think of that?" is going to go over pretty well and will perk up his ears. Here, I tell my clients to use me as a scapegoat and throw in a little humor to keep it light. Susie can say something like, "This Stress Therapist lady, Cheri Flake, has a system called "the Love List" that seems pretty simple. She says that it will stop all my nagging and get us on the ball with all that we have to do around the house without us even talking about it! I know you'd like that, right?" Or, "Seems like it doesn't involve much, wanna try it?" Or, "This lady says that she has some simple way to eliminate all nagging! Less work, less arguing and no more nagging sounds awesome. Want to give it a shot?"

Joey, if you're reading this and want the Love List to be a part of your relationship, I will assume that you feel unappreciated, are tired of what seems like constant nagging and are ready for a change. Although I rarely see you bring the Love List to your spouse's attention, there is no reason why you shouldn't. If you are the one raising the subject with Susie, your focus needs to be on the fact that there is a new and simple way to get all the household tasks done with much less work for her. If Susie has been basically running the household already, it's important that you don't inadvertently criticize her way of doing things. Rather, Joey will emphasize that he wants to try using a new way to communicate about what needs attention and with clear deadlines. Keep it simple, Joey: "Susie, you won't have to constantly remind me anymore to do things around the house!" is a nice place to start.

Regardless of who initiates the Love List, it is imperative that both partners share the attitude, feeling and energy of joint desire and good humor. Remember, you both *want* this! You want this for you, each other and your relationship. This is not "I read this book so you must!" or "I know this better and we're supposed to do it this way." The spirit is more experimental, and even playful: "I don't know what she means, or even if this will work, but what if it does?"

On a side note, when deciding on a good time to bring up the Love List, it is always better to have important discussions when things are going very well between the two of you. A lot of my clients find this relatively difficult, because when things are going well, they're afraid to bring up something that might be met with anything other than a cooperative attitude. However, this is *absolutely* when you need to bring up any new concerns. Issues brought up when there is tension, and certainly during a full-blown fight, are charged with resentment rather than love. Your own experience bears this out. How often has "Oh! And another thing...!" gone well in an argument? Probably never.

Remember, once you get started, using the Love List system is going to be very, very simple. The reason it is laid out here so carefully and in such detail is not because of any inherent complexity, but rather to make sure you have everything you need to make the system work right the first time and forever.

Things to Know:

✓ The couple must act as a team when implementing the Love List.

✓ The Love List is innately simple. The only reason it is laid out here so carefully is to ensure that the couple's first stab at it is a successful one.

Things to Do

✓ Present the Love List to your partner by discussing how it will benefit your partner, not you.

The Prep

Now that you have brought up the Love List, it's time to schedule a couples meeting, marital meeting, love meeting or whatever the couple chooses to call it. Make it clear that the meeting's only purpose is to set out the ground rules in a very limited time, no more than ten to fifteen minutes. This short investment of time will reward the two of you greatly: No more nagging or talking about all of the boring household tasks or the division of labor anymore! The "Honey Do" list will finally be done!

Susie, remember, Joey will not want to discuss the subject at length having had absolutely no time to think it over. So do not try to engage for long. Just get the meeting on the shared calendar (and if you don't have one, I'll cover that later) and move on. "Hey, remember that book about no more nagging? I want to try it, cool if we talk about it on Friday after the kids go to bed? I'll put it on our calendar, say, at 8:30pm?" Between this decision to schedule and the actual meeting, do not mention the Love List or the meeting again. If Joey has agreed to meet, great. Consider it done. Mentioning it again is just another form of nagging.

Joey, for Susie, the message that you are thinking of her and of a way to enhance your relationship and teamwork will probably be received with pleasant compliance. You should have no problem getting this on the agenda and setting a meeting time. When you tell Susie that you have an idea on how to get all of the little jobs done around the house, Susie will be delighted and will probably put hearts and stars around the designated meeting calendar day.

As a side note, I highly recommend that all couples set up a shared digital calendar. Access to a shared calendar can make life way easier and is simple to set up. A quick Google search can get you started, or better yet, throw this item on the next Love List.

It is a good idea to schedule the meeting within one week of its being mentioned. You want it to remain important, not something that can be easily blown off. Meetings scheduled two or three weeks out tend to lose their impact. By the same token, same-day scheduled meetings tend to feel like criticism. Any covert hostility associated with the meeting might detract from your focus and ultimately thwart your good intentions.

For the same reasons, know that if absolutely necessary you can reschedule the first meeting, but you must reschedule it at the next earliest opportunity and in no event more than a week out. "Have a plan, but be flexible" is the mantra of the Love List, and you can start chanting this from the start. A "plan" needs a date and a time. While the particulars of the plan may change, there is always one in place.

The theory behind the Love List is that always having a plan in place is the key to success and the initial meeting set-up is the platform for this new practice. Why is a plan that you ultimately may change so important? Our brains are very forgiving when we have a plan and not so when we do not, *even if we end up having to change the plan.* We just don't feel bad about a disorganized basement if we have a plan to tackle it this weekend at a scheduled time. When we have a plan, we actually feel good about the task which in turn, inspires our brain to allow us to start digging into the holiday decorations deep in the depths of the basement come Saturday morning.

If, while you are discussing the meeting, the Love List, or any related process, you hear any concerns or reservations from your partner, do not ignore them. Instead, engage with your partner and even acknowledge or agree with the sentiment, but make sure to *still follow through with the plan.* "I know it's tough to meet this week but it'll only be a few minutes. She says in the book that we need to meet within a week of discussing it...that's weird, but let's just roll with it." Don't stick up for me (I can take it!) or do anything that misaligns the two of you. It's time for you two to be a team!

For simplicity, I will assume from here on out that Susie is the one bringing the Love List to the relationship. Therefore, once the meeting is scheduled, Susie has two tasks and Joey has none. Seems unfair, I know. But, remember, the payoff for Susie is enormous, and making it as simple as possible for Joey is key for the Love List to work. Susie's two tasks are to set up an inbox system and to create the couple's first Love List.

Things to Know:

✓ The Love List will be received best if brought up when things are going well between the couple.

✓ Regardless of who brings up the Love List, the initial discussion needs to be brief, undertaken with a lighthearted attitude, and conducted with the other's benefits in mind.

Things to Do:

✓ After discussing what the Love List is, schedule a couples meeting within one week. Agree you will limit your initial meeting time to ten to fifteen minutes, and stick to this limit.

✓ During all discussions regarding the Love List, stay aligned as a team.

The Inbox System

First, Susie must put together an inbox system for the couple. It's as easy as using spaces that already exist (some kitchens and office furniture come with a built-in office with slots for this) or just buying two paper trays (available in the office/organization section in most stores). You are fine as long as there are two spaces accessible and designated for both Susie and Joey. Keep it simple: One for Susie. One for Joey. This is where the Love List will live.

Many of my clients report already having this type of system in place. However, it is imperative that both parties agree to use it! Obtaining agreement to use the inbox system will actually be a main focus of the initial meeting. As an alternate form of communication between the couple, the inboxes or trays will be the way each of you "listen" to one another. You will find this type of system yields a multitude of other incidental benefits, including simpler and easier communication with your partner, but it is absolutely essential for the Love List to work.

Susie, prior to the first meeting, designate the area where the inbox system will reside. Pick a high-traffic area that is neutral for *both* parties. If you don't see it, you won't check it. This is why the kitchen tends to be the most ideal location. Make this decision on your own for now, and make a note that during the first meeting, you will discuss the location of the inbox system. It may prove to be very important to your partner.

Even before meeting, Susie can go ahead and introduce the inbox system to Joey and start *using* it! Let Joey know that he has an inbox now, and *briefly* mention that it pertains to the Love List and that you will be putting all of his mail in it from now on. This way, to get his mail he will need to check it. If he normally gets the mail, take over this task for a bit. It is very important that Joey is eventually checking his inbox with regularity so it becomes habitual. Again, for now, just let him know that the inboxes are there, that they have to do with the Love List (do *not* mention your meeting!), and you will be placing mail in them. Save the particulars of the actual Love List system for the meeting.

Incidentally, if you think that the introduction of the inbox system will go over better during the initial meeting, that is fine. However, do not underestimate the power of a little-by-little approach when initiating change. Because motivation comes after action, using the inboxes before the meeting may get the both of you excited about more changes to come.

Although the easiest way that you can create the habit of checking your inbox is by placing the mail in it, you can certainly get creative in the various ways that you get Joey to check it. Put things in there you know he will need to retrieve in order to go about his daily business, like his keys if they are misplaced or a number that you know he'll need soon. There are no hard and fast rules. Put a chocolate or a piece of licorice in there if you have to! The goal is to eventually have the Love List magically become just another piece of paper in the inbox to address regularly.

Make your inbox a fun and productive place to hang out. The incidental benefits of an inbox system are vast. Small issues that are quick and easy, and therefore not really worthy of the Love List now but were probably ignored in the past, are now a snap! Items that might just need validation, opinion or provide information have a place in the inbox. "I decided on this camp" attached to a summer camp brochure. Even a "Pretty cool, huh? What do you think?" may elicit a validating, "Cool!" written beneath this note and placed back in your inbox. No more lonely decision making, or items that were never "discussed." Now, there is input on both sides and everybody feels supported and valued.

Most importantly, life has become just a bit easier. Remember, your brain loves habits and wants everything to be as automatic as taking a shower. Thus, repetitive behaviors will have your brain clamoring for more. This is why your brain thinks that *Instagram* or *Words with Friends* or even your email is so incredibly important. The repeated checking behavior day in and day out reinforces a pressing message to your brain and within no time at all your brain is convinced, "*Facebook* is *very* important!" Habitual behaviors not only seem important, but also are innately stress-free allowing the behavior to be quite uneventful. We want Joey to really get that the inbox is as imperative but as comfortable as checking football scores. Even better, he will begin to see firsthand that the two of you don't have to verbally discuss many household matters at all. You are basically introducing a system in which both of you know that items and tasks are part of a plan that establishes an open line of communication that is non-verbal and immune to nagging and resentment.

I cannot stress enough that both of you need to check your inbox and address its contents regularly and deal with, discard or file whatever is in there. Do not leave something in there unaddressed for long. Eventually, any ignored item will cause stress. Your brain doesn't know the difference between a big commitment or a small commitment to do something. If you blow it off, the stress is the same. If something is in your inbox, from now on you file, deal, plan or do.

It is also important that our brain does not associate the inbox with a flux of unaddressed items. This association is dangerous indeed! Our brains avoid tasks and behaviors that we believe will be difficult or boring. To avoid this pitfall, be sure to put fun, kind, humorous and even flirty notes in his inbox. If Joey is way into his garden right now, throw a coupon for the local nursery in his box with a sticky note that says, "Thought you might like this!" Got a private joke? Allude to it on a quick note to Joey to make him smile. Just a little something funny that happened that day on a sticky note can brighten your spouse's day. And, if he's smiling he'll be much more likely to follow through on other obligations that might not be as fun.

In order to make the system as simple as possible, as well as evoke a desire to be compliant and actually use the system, you'll need to have easy access to items that facilitate using the inboxes. Stock up on the "school supplies" that the two of you will need to keep the inboxes moving. Pens, sticky notes, a stapler and maybe even scissors and tape readily available make it easy and enjoyable to communicate in this way. Keep your school supplies organized and right next to the inbox *so you will use them*. Not being able to find a pen is an easy way to miss out on an otherwise sweet or productive thought.

When selecting your supplies and arranging the inbox location, pay attention to each of your personal preferences in how you correspond. This preference point is more important than we tend to think. Are you more of a pencil person or a marker person? Have what appeals to you and Joey and both of you will be more likely to use it. For years, my husband's favorite thing to write with was a particular brand of fine, blue, felt-tip marker. One of the first things I did when I set up our system was to keep four or five of them right next to our inboxes. This was a sweet and subtle way to encourage talking to me in this old school, pre-millennial and even romantic way.

Things to Know:

✓ Susie will be the one to set up the inbox system during the time between the bring-up and the couple's initial meeting.

✓ The inbox system is comprised of two trays: One for Joey and one for Susie. They are placed in a neutral location where the couple can exchange paper documents.

✓ Joey and Susie will both check the inbox frequently until

doing so becomes habitual. This new communication method depends on consistency from both sides.

Things to Do:

✓ Susie, decide where your inbox system will be located, set it up, tell Joey about it and begin using it!

✓ Susie, feel free to get creative regarding ways to get Joey to check the inbox frequently.

The Love List

Onward to the next and final task before the big meeting! Susie will be the one to make the first actual Love List for Joey. The Love List will be created in a Word or Pages document or whatever digital format works for both Joey and Susie. Susie will construct two columns: On the left: "I am happy to…" and on the right: "By this date, honey!" She titles it, "Joey's Love List" and proceeds to fill it in. To help get you started, I've included a Sample Love List at the end of this book.

It is important that Susie starts with five to eight items. These can range from things that need to be done within the next day or two to tasks that have due dates pretty far out there. Later, when it is all old hat, you can move it to ten items, but limit it to ten at the most. Keep a note for yourself containing items that didn't make the Love List this time around. You can include them on subsequent Love Lists.

I like adding items that aren't imperative but that I still want to keep on the radar. I have a couple like, "Download box of our CDs to iTunes" that have a due date that is longer than a year away!

These long away due date items will give Joey a sense of control and calmness. After all, this one is a year away…I don't have to hear nagging about this until after a year goes by!? Yes!!! And it gives him choice and control over when and how to accomplish the items and plan his schedule.

It is also important that Susie puts some very easily handled items on the Love List like, "Change the lightbulb in the laundry room." As my kids would say, such items are "easy breezy lemon squeezy"-- they are quickly and handily checked off and for that reason, will empower Joey and make him feel productive, motivated to keep it up and feeling more like the "man of the house." (No kidding. I have had this reported to me a lot).

If you have a hot topic, that is, an item that has been nagged to death or is a predictable trigger for the big fight, it's best to avoid listing this item on the first Love List. After all, both Joey and Susie need to like the Love List in order for it work. Any item that is associated with dread or perhaps even anger needs to stay off for a bit. If "Sell that damn car!" has been on one of the old "Honey Do" lists for months and months, it can wait a few more weeks. Also, Susie now has an opportunity to break the task up into simple ones so it all doesn't seem like such a drag to Joey. To get the ball rolling, she may include small incremental actions items on the Love List: "Check Kelley Blue Book on the car," or "Pick up an Auto Trader ~ Do we want to list the car here?" The added bonus of asking Joey a question *that you are actually wondering about* and that needs his input will let him know his opinion is valued. It may also inspire him to move on an otherwise dormant project.

For her part, Susie has the chance to use the Love List to engage on the same project. She might include a request like "Send me all the stats and a pic of the car and I'll post it on the neighborhood list serve." The Love List gets the stats written and photos taken, and in no time at all, the couple is working as a team!

Susie needs to really keep in mind Joey's schedule, preferences, abilities and habits when she assigns the deadlines. Remember, upon receipt of the Love List, Joey will be able to edit them, but I have found that when the deadlines are realistic, he does so far less often. Go ahead and avoid any extraneous back and forth by being thoughtful and courteous in assigning a due date. If Joey's brother is in town this weekend, perhaps the following weekend would be better to fix the hammock. If Joey works late on Mondays and is usually spent and overtired, don't add a bunch of items with Tuesday due dates.

Know that it does not matter if the items are just "little things." Our brains don't know the difference between, "Today I will buy this house" and, "Today I will dust this fan." To our brain, it is all BIG. Failing to do it feels bad even if it's small. And our brains will do anything to avoid feeling bad, which can sabotage the system.

One of the ways that I have added to the Love List over the years is by color coding particular items. Color signals that something needs specific attention or further clarification.

Red may be the first color that you add to your Love List, used where an item is overdue. It is of critical importance to communicate clearly when items have not been completed by the due date. These red-coded items, by definition, have fallen into the "Nag Zone" and are open for discussion and verbal reminders, i.e., nagging. Even if the nag-able item isn't in red font, as you can see on the Sample Love List, it is still very clearly marked. I use the phase "DANGER, NAG ALERT!" but of course feel free to express this sentiment in your own way.

The beauty of the Love List is that until an item on it has been ignored and is past its due date, the assigning spouse does not even mention it. On the flip side of this deal, if a deadline does pass without having been renegotiated, the item may be changed to red and a license to nag has been issued! And by the way, be sure to list the Nag Alerts last so it's not the first thing Joey sees when he opens the document. Remember, he has to *like* the Love List for it to work.

As our household Love List has progressed over the years and other needs have arisen, I have gradually included more color coding. Pink means we need to do a task together as a couple. We will have to schedule it on our shared family calendar or perhaps I have already added it. Orange means "I'm not sure if this was done because the communication was unclear," or "Some completion is evident, but it still needs attention," or "You may have missed this, did you?" and so on. I use purple to indicate that the item must be completed by TODAY. This is a rare inclusion, and one I suggest you omit from most of your Love Lists (and certainly from your first few). I use it only rarely myself, when it is absolutely necessary — say, when our goldfish are in dire straits and need attention that very day.

The most recent addition I have made is a blue-coded "Just so you know…" category. Maybe it's because I am a therapist, but at our house, we express our needs. Not to say there is no spontaneity, but in general, if you want flowers, it is OK to ask for flowers. If you want a specific kind of flower, you mention it. It may *sound* unromantic, but I have found in my home and with my clients that in practice, it is quite wonderful and *truly* romantic. "I told him my needs and he met them!" is a way better feeling than, "I was hoping he would do this and he didn't," any way you cut it. Blue items can serve as subtle reminders that when expressed verbally can sound a lot like nagging. A quick, "Your mom's birthday is on Thursday" just feels kind and considerate in print and keeps the "I swear I told you a hundred times!" argument at bay.

I cannot reiterate enough however, that when starting out, simpler is *always* better. Especially in your first few go-rounds, you should focus on getting used to the system and using it consistently. For this reason, the Sample Love List that I have provided is a basic one without color or a key. However, after the two of you are rolling along with your newly established system and a few Love Lists have made the rounds, you may want to color some items and provide a key for detail and clarity. If you are using the Sample Love List as a guide, you can imagine which items might be color coded and how this enhancement may work for your household in the future.

Part of the deal of course is that Susie will need to keep the Love List current. If I falter and casually mention something that needs to be done around the house, my husband can justifiably suggest that I put it on the Love List, and then check out. I myself have to be sure to check the Love List regularly and get it to him because not only have I made an agreement to do so but, get this...he actually *prefers* the Love List! I suggest that Susie has a pop-up reminder weekly or bi-weekly to check on the list and then she can easily get it over to Joey in a timely manner.

What I like the most about the the Love List is that everyone is accountable, even Susie. This accountability and the structure of a shared system makes the couple feel truly like a team.

There is one more issue for Susie to address before the initial meeting -- whether Susie will decide to give Joey this book to read in advance. This depends on whether your Joey is the type of person who would be okay with this much content and not feel overwhelmed. Certainly, ignore this suggestion if you think he may find it a burden, annoying or pushy. No one knows Joey like Susie! My Joey would want to read this book, but many Joeys would not -- and you don't want to lose him before you even get started!

If you decide that your Joey would want to read the book first, send it along via his inbox with a no-nag note that says something like, "FYI: Regarding the Love List" or, "Read this before our meeting on Friday, if you get the chance."

Things to Know:

✓ Susie will be the one who creates the Love List in a digital format for Joey.

✓ The simpler the first Love List is, the more likely it will be adopted. It is five to eight tasks with clear deadlines and possibly a key for clarity.

✓ Unless the due date on a particular item has passed without being renegotiated, it is off-limits for discussion. If that does occur, it has fallen into the "Nag Zone," is clearly labeled, and may even appear in red. It is also fair game for discussion and verbal follow-up.

Things to Do:

✓ Susie, create the Love List in a digital document, print out a copy for each of you and have it ready for the meeting.

✓ Susie, decide whether giving *Honey Do to Honey DONE!* to Joey to read *before* the meeting will improve its quality. If you think this will get him fired up, pass this book along to him via his inbox.

The Meeting

At the initial meeting, stay positive, be brief, and keep the big picture in mind. Remember, you are joining *with your partner* in this endeavor. Again, one of you has brought the Love List to the attention of the other, and it's important that discussing it further does not turn into another argument. Rather than go into it, just try to convince your partner that you both need to do this with a curious and experimental attitude. A casual "Hmm. This lady seems to know her stuff, let's give this a try. What if it works?" attitude will get the conversation rolling with no one feeling alienated. Bring this book as a reference to provide some clarity as needed.

Open with the purpose: to make sure that both parties understand and agree to what their responsibilities will be, what the Love List is specifically, and how it will all go down. Susie, it is important that you keep in mind for the duration of the meeting that your goal is only to introduce a new method of communication to Joey, one that will cease all nagging. If the meeting runs too long, or there is more discussion than is necessary to get the system in place, you run the risk of making the meeting itself a nagging session or worse, somehow being construed as more criticism. Better to get the system rolling first. You can tweak and refine it later along the lines I have suggested in this book.

Susie quickly follows this statement of purpose by addressing the inbox system and explaining how it works if the couple hasn't been using it already. Come to an agreement that the inbox system is not optional or occasional, but is *integral* to the Love List and therefore will be addressed with *frequent* regularity. Regularity in this context means checking it on *most* days. Both parties must follow through on this contract to use the inbox system as it is imperative for the Love List to be successful.

If you have already been using the inbox, Susie can then address, discuss and resolve relevant questions so both parties continue to use and benefit from it. "How's it going?" "Do you like it?" "Is the location okay?" Susie can make a few notes and then, immediately following the meeting, make any necessary changes to the inbox system.

Susie may want to mention that the more often each spouse checks the inbox, the less time it takes to handle the items inside. It is imperative that the inbox is not seen in and of itself as a time-consuming chore. Our brains avoid things that take up too much of our valuable time, so checking the inbox will need to be construed as a super quick job.

Next, Susie will need to have a copy of their first Love List for

Joey take a look at while she explains how it works.

Things to Know:

✓ The goal of the initial meeting is to introduce a new communication system that ceases all nagging.

✓ The initial meeting will need to be kept under fifteen minutes -- ten to fifteen minutes is typical -- and have a casual, positive and "all defenses down" feel.

Things to Do:

✓ If the couple isn't already using the inbox system, Susie will first explain the system as simply as possible.

✓ Acknowledging that the inboxes are the key to the Love List and its ultimate success, the couple will agree to use it regularly and check it on most days.

✓ Susie will note any agreed changes that come up regarding the inboxes and implement them immediately following the meeting.

✓ Susie, have your first Love List printed out and ready to go.

The Process

During the initial meeting, the process of how exactly the Love List works is laid out clearly for Joey. Susie explains to Joey that within one day after the meeting, she will email the Love List to him. The subject line will read: "Love List - Please confirm that you have received this." When Joey gets it, he simply replies with, "Got it." This simple exchange gets rid of any muddy, "Not sure if you heard me," or wondering "Did he get it?" concerns. Communication is clear and concise.

Joey's confirmed receipt not only communicates automatic responsibility for the list but also starts a clock ticking. Joey has one week from the time of his confirmation email back to Susie to print out the Love List, mark it up, edit target dates if need be, and get it back to Susie via her inbox. If for some reason he cannot meet this deadline, Joey must send Susie an email specifying the date within a week that he will have the Love List in her box. Later on, when things are rolling along nicely, a strict one-week deadline probably won't be necessary, but it is nice at the beginning to get in the habit of using the new system.

Joey, be kind in sending your email confirming that you got the Love List. Don't try to blow this off for a bit so you have a longer time to turn it around. After a few go arounds, the Love List will be so simple and will take only a few minutes to review and return. Think of Susie's hard work on the front end, and send her the email that you got it within a day or so. Validate Susie by letting her know that you are on board with this plan with a simple email and two words, "Got it!" Now is your time to shine, Joey!

Susie then retrieves the hard copy Love List from her inbox. She pulls up the original document electronically and moves any changes that Joey has provided on the hard copy to her file. Susie then has one week to email the updated Love List back to Joey and it all repeats again. That's it! The Love List is officially in business!

Keep in mind that Susie has to address any concern that Joey may have noted with respect to a specific item or a thought that has just been scribbled in the margin. If there are concerns that can't be edited on the Love List itself, she will answer them on paper and place the response in Joey's inbox. For example, say there is an item on the Love List for Joey to switch out a car seat and he has completed this item but has written next to it, "When does he move to a booster seat? Do you know?" Susie can write on a piece of paper, "Regarding a booster for Joey Jr., it looks like it will be a while…I looked it up, Booster seats are recommended for children 4-7 years old who are less than 4 feet 9 inches tall" and throw the note in Joey's inbox. This is a nice, casual, no blame, no nag exchange. The car seat was installed, the information was shared, no one is mad, and Junior is safe and sound.

The markups entail Joey's crossing off items that were completed or negotiating new due dates for items that weren't completed or for some reason cannot be completed by the date Susie initially provided. It's important for Susie to do all she can to avoid an inflexible due date, as the opportunity for Joey to change due dates is one of the most alluring things about the Love List. However, if there is a date that is hard and fast for some reason, that date needs to be added to Susie's key in some way or explained in parentheses after the task. For example, if the car needs to be serviced before a vacation, Susie can include this item along with a due date *two weeks before the trip* and use an identifier in the description to express the urgency. This way, Joey still has a bit of time and flexibility to change the date if need be. Susie might write: "Car serviced for our trip to Florida!" on the left and "March 15th (we're leaving on April 1st)" on the right. Incidentally, a coupon for a service at a particular business may be placed in Joey's box with a note, "Per Love List car service item." Know that handing him the coupon can feel like nagging. Don't do it. You have the inbox, so use it instead.

At the initial meeting, after explaining the process involved with the Love List, Susie will need to add that this is the *only* time that they will discuss these items that are currently listed on it verbally. From now on, all communication, changes, completions and additions will be electronic or hand-written on the Love List itself and delivered electronically by Susie or manually by Joey via Susie's inbox. The only exception to this communication system is that it may be brought up in subsequent meetings. By "brought up" I mean the *process* of the Love List, not the items listed on it. Those are off limits and cannot be verbally discussed unless they are have moved into the Nag Zone on the Love List itself. One tip: When Susie sends the most current Love List, she can include a date after the title to make it clear for Joey which version is the latest and greatest (for example, "Love List 5-2-16"). He need only keep a copy of the most current version.

There is something fundamentally wonderful about Susie being the one to explain that all verbal communication regarding tasks that she likely has been nagging about is over. It implies that she understands this well and will follow through on the no-nag promise. This can leave quite an impression on Joey and have him really wanting the Love List system to work as well.

Things to Know:

✓ Now that the inbox system has been explained, Susie shows the Love List to Joey and explains the process and how it will all go down.

✓ The process works like this: Susie emails the Love List to Joey within a day after the meeting. When Joey receives the Love List, he is to send a quick email back to Susie confirming that he got it. Joey now has one week to print it out, complete relevant items, manually write notes or edit deadlines and get a hard copy back to Susie via her inbox. Susie edits it with the new changes and sends it back via email to Joey within one week and the process starts over…This exchange is how the Love List stays in business.

Things to Do:

✓   Susie, explain the Love List to Joey and how it will work.

✓   Susie, end the Love List discussion by explaining to Joey that from now on, verbally discussing any item on the Love List that has not fallen into the Nag Zone is strictly prohibited.

The Agreement

The ultimate goal of the initial meeting is to not only encourage the use of the inbox system and explain the process of the Love List, but to have both parties then agree to be accountable and *use* the system as it has been laid out here. The agreement doesn't need to be formal, but a verbal contract that both parties promise to give it a shot and follow the rules is necessary. A promise is a promise, after all.

Part of the agreement must include the initial strict one-week deadline to move the Love List back and forth. Just to make this easy, I recommend to my clients that they pick a particular day each week that this reminder pops up. The Love List eventually gets only a couple of minutes (and believe it or not, sometimes *only* a minute) of attention and then it's off to the other partner. When things are rolling along nicely, you can loosen up the deadline, but I highly recommend that the Love List makes an appearance in both Joey and Susie's life at least every two weeks or it will be quickly be reconsidered, perhaps determined to no longer be important and therefore, easily forgotten and ultimately blown off.

After Joey and Susie agree that the Love List is their new communication system, they can also agree from now on to only bring up issues and concerns on the Love List itself, via the inbox, or in a follow-up meeting (I'll cover subsequent meetings in the next section). All must be considered as *very important* to avoid the whole system losing momentum and becoming energy wasted on one more thing that "didn't work for us."

When you have addressed the inboxes, explained the Love List, and secured these basic agreements, the meeting is over. Do not linger or engage in any overtime *even if you are engaging in conversation that is irrelevant to the Love List.* If the last ten minutes of the meeting were about weekend plans or funny things that happened at work this week, the meeting may still register with Joey, even unconsciously, as ten minutes longer than planned (or desired!). This negative association leaves the meeting in danger of being labeled as a time burden and possibly avoided in the future. This is so dangerous, in fact, that I recommend that Susie has an engagement "that she must attend to" immediately following the meeting to avoid this trap. It is natural. Because you love each other, if you aren't used to putting some time aside to engage in casual talk and fun, you'll likely keep rolling with it the first time that you do. If you observe this may be happening toward the end of the meeting, you may want to say, "Ok, cool, I gotta run but it looks like we got this…if we have any questions we can just meet again…same time next week?" Blow a kiss, exit, and it's done.

Susie, if you feel like the two of you are really enjoying the dedicated time together during the initial meeting, perhaps you may also want schedule some separate connection time on your shared calendar. Incidentally, couples that plan to talk at certain times or schedule sex are more likely to talk and have sex. Now, I should also say that if the meeting runs ten minutes over because you are making out, this will probably strengthen Joey's attendance probability, making all my points about the meeting being a "time burden" moot! There are exceptions to every rule, and Susie, you know your man better than anyone. Just remember who you are meeting with at all times.

Things to Know:

✓ The ultimate goal of the initial meeting is to encourage the use of the inbox system, explain the process of the Love List and *agree to use it* just as it is laid out here. After the couple has achieved this, the meeting is over. No overtime allowed.

✓ It is important the Love List be considered important and worth a try by *both* Joey and Susie for it to have success.

✓ Keep up the one-week deadline in returning the Love List to one another for a while before loosening up so the process becomes habitual.

✓ The more often you address the Love List, the quicker and easier it will become.

Things to Do:

✓ Schedule a time each week to review the Love List for new additions.

✓ Joey and Susie, verbally agree to give the Love List a shot, bring up issues if you have them via the inbox or subsequent meetings, and consider the process an important part of your communication as a couple.

The Check-In

If this meeting goes well, and it's under fifteen minutes, go ahead and mention that a weekly meeting may be in order. Inquire to see if there is an interest in regular weekly meetings just to touch base about things generally. Keep this inquiry vague and remind Joey that this will not be a nagging session because *that is over!* Remember, even at regularly scheduled meetings, Joey and Susie may bring up process-related issues with the Love List, but not specific Love List tasks. Verbal discussion is strictly prohibited on these items unless they have been moved into the Nag Zone.

If at first regular meetings are frowned upon for some reason, don't sweat it, Susie. For now, schedule one check-in meeting for a week or two out just so you have an outlet to gripe, praise, question or just give each other high fives.

Please know, however, that I highly recommend that couples have a weekly meeting set up in their shared calendar. Sure, it is great to address the Love List questions that may come up, but even better to have the scheduled time to just touch base and talk. If couples don't talk regularly, they will only hear pressing complaints from their partners. I love hearing about my husband's good days and getting a chance to run some ideas past him about my business or cool stories about the kids. Now that he has been exposed to the good that can come from these meetings, my husband really values this time as well. I know this to be true because when we don't have it, he requests it.

Weekly meetings or subsequent meetings must not be seen as one more thing that you have to do, or you will dread and avoid them just like anything you feel bad about. One way to keep the meetings productive and fun is to keep a list on your phone (if you have an iPhone, the app called Notes works well) as things come up from day-to-day that you'd like to include during the meeting. Sometimes this is just a joke you heard, a funny story at work or a decision you'd like your better half to weigh in on. If there is nothing to discuss, go ahead and make out for the ten or fifteen minutes, talk about a book you're reading, look at pictures from a recent vacation, or do something else fun!

Things to Know:

- ✓ Meetings are for process-related concerns, not to address specific tasks on the Love List.

- ✓ I highly recommend regularly scheduled meetings for couples to check in, not only about the Love List, but about anything at all. These meetings open up communication in all other areas and thereby strengthen the relationship.

Things to Do:

✓   Susie, at the close of the initial meeting, schedule a check-in meeting to ensure everything is going well and to clear up any concerns regarding the Love List.

✓   Susie, feel out Joey regarding a regular weekly or bi-weekly meeting just for the two of you to check in, talk or make-out.

The Rub

Clients always ask me why there is only one Love List and not two, that is, in addition to the Love List from Susie to Joey, a second Love List from Joey to Susie only seems fair. Let me start by saying that you're welcome to initiate the Two-Way Love List System. Go for it! But only do so after you've been using the Love List in its traditional format for at least several months. This way, the Love List will have already become habitual and you won't run the risk of making it too cumbersome for your brain right off the bat, which leads to avoidance. The more complicated the Love List gets, the less likely you'll be to use it, and it is better to have a one-way Love List working for you than no Love List at all.

I must add that in my years of teaching the Love List, I have yet to see anyone who really needs two Love Lists. Why is this? I think after using the Love List for a bit, both parties find that they are actually getting all that they want from it. It may sound fairer to have two Love Lists going back and forth, as a way to please all parties, but after one Love List has been going strong, a second rarely justifies the additional effort. Although nagging itself may be a two-way street, in my practice a one-way Love List seems to do the trick, whether one finds themselves a nagger or a nag-ee. In practice, it seems that there is always one person, usually the primary caregiver and/or homemaker, i.e., Susie, who just doesn't need one. Since Susies tend to be more in tune with what needs to be done around the house and for the family, they probably already have some sort of system in place to handle it all, making an incoming Love List moot. Joey can simply add any items to Susie's inbox, and she will likely take it from there.

The initial agreement to *use* the Love List, and then the actual follow up and accountability on both sides to follow through with the agreed upon plan, open up the lines of communication. A mutual respect arises. Neither person can or wants to slack off, not only because it increases the likelihood that their own needs won't be met, but also because using the List becomes fun and satisfying. You are helping your partner out in ways that they have identified, and doing so without nagging, without resentment, and in a spirit of respect and love.

Things to Know:

✓ If you perceive a compelling need for two Love Lists, wait until you have first implemented one Love List with success for at least several months. Having the basic Love List behaviors become habitual is more important at first than adding a second Love List.

✓ Although it may seem unfair in theory, in practice, one Love List gets the job done and will most often render two Love

Lists unnecessary.

Things to Do:

✓   If you are thinking of using two Love Lists, calendar a date several months out to reevaluate this necessity, once you have given yourself time to make one Love List a part of your routine.

The Concerns

As you embark on the Love List, I want you to be 100% convinced and excited about the new possibilities for your relationship. So let's talk about a few of the concerns I hear frequently, and that you may be asking yourself now. In no particular order, they are:

1. "I'm not sure I can get used to the idea of never discussing the Love List items. Do you really mean it when you say we never, ever talk about them again?"

What we normally do feels the most comfortable to our brains. Discussing day-to-day household items, though disruptive, is how you normally operate, so the idea of stopping this behavior may give your brain a start. Don't panic. What you are doing now is not working. Discussions that feel like criticism lead to arguments and nagging. When you are asking questions via the Love List, communication is clear and this will make you feel like a team. When you are functioning as a team, love and respect is present.

That being said, I have occasionally gotten a Love List back from my husband with an item circled and that says, "Let's discuss." This implies that the Love List won't work for this item. If Joey is requesting to talk about a particular item, he won't see it as nagging when you bring it up and he may even casually bring it up himself.

2. "He hasn't been checking his inbox. I can see that it's full."

Before getting upset about an overfull inbox, try enticing him to check it. Put something in there that he finds hilarious, irresistible or even sexy. A joke, a favorite piece of candy or a love note with a quick, "Did you get my special treat? It's in your inbox…" may get him back in business. If, despite humor and enticements, one partner is not checking the inbox with enough regularity, schedule a meeting on your shared calendar to talk about what the problem may be. Keep it light and ask questions. It may be something simple like the location, or he may simply apologize and agree again to check it regularly because he knows it means something to you, *not because it gets you upset*. Getting upset starts to look and feel a lot like nagging.

3. "If he doesn't send me a confirm receipt when I send the Love List, can I send it again?"

Absolutely. I would wait two or three days. If you don't hear back after a second send, say to him, "I sent you a Love List, did you get it?" Then, "You know, you're supposed to send me an email saying that you got it…" and walk away. Give him a chance to remedy his mistake by seeing how he does the next time.

4. "It takes him longer than a week to get the Love List back to me. Should I schedule a meeting?"

This may be a "pick your battles" moment. Is he getting it back to you in two weeks? In nine days? Who cares?! If he is getting the job done in a reasonable time, you may casually mention this at the next meeting but ask yourself what you really want…Do you want him to use the Love List, or do you want him to strictly follow the one-week rule? I know one thing for sure; *you don't want him to hate the Love List.* Since the Love List is actually working and the goal is to get off the hard and fast deadline and eventually make the process automatic, you may want to roll with it.

5. "I have an item that is in the "Nag Zone." So do I just start nagging?"

It's true you now have a license to nag, but I would try humor first. A prize that you get to be mean is not much of a prize, and a check-in first will usually get the job done. I usually say something like, "How's the office cleaning project coming along?" You can nag, but you may learn that you don't have to anymore. A simple, "You know, all you have to do is change the date on that," may suffice.

6. "Can't we just move the Love List exclusively to electronic correspondence instead of using the paper and inbox?"

You may, but wait a few months. It's nice to get used to using the inbox and addressing the Love List in a structured way first. Making these behaviors habitual is the key to long-term success. Plus, if you move to electronic only, it may squelch the need for an inbox and you may miss all the productivity and fun that can come with an inbox system.

7. "I have shared or "Family Reminders" on my iPhone, can't we just use this instead of a Love List?"

Probably not yet and not for a while, if ever. This is more like "Cheri Flake Stress Therapy Graduate School." Unless you've been seeing me for a while or have a really mastered the Love List process and techniques as described in this book, you're probably in "Cheri Flake Stress Therapy 101." Incorporating the Love List itself into shared reminders is a very advanced way of using the Love List and presents challenges even for the Love List power user. Best to start out simply as I've explained here, and when you've graduated from "Cheri Flake University," that is, you have read this book and have been successfully following my advice for some time, then give it a try.

8. "This won't work. He just won't do it."

I would schedule a meeting and discuss this concern. Stick to your feelings about the effort you have already expended, and ask him what you can do to help him participate. See if he needs something more from you. Tell him this means something to you. Certainly, you want to do your best to clear up any hurt feelings or emotionally charged items before you put a Love List in place. If you get upset and start fighting, the Love List will fall to the wayside. Where the level of animosity is just too high, or some other issues is a persistent impediment, perhaps you could benefit from a few sessions with a counselor.

9. "I'm not sure I can do this alone...explaining it all and following up...it's a lot! Can you help me?"

Yes. I am here always. Please feel free to send any questions or concerns to me through my website at www.TheStressTherapist.com.

The Send Off

You've got this! If you need help, I am here, but you are now armed and ready for a way more productive household, and an easier, more joyful life with your partner.

Good luck! I wish you a long happy life of no more nagging, a joyful relationship, a productive household and a lifetime of Honey Do to Honey DONE!

Much love and light to you and yours,

Cheri

Sample Love List:

Joey's Love List
March 30, 2016

It's easy for me to...	by this date, honey!
Clean aquarium	TODAY
Sort books for book drive	This weekend? Added to Shared calendar for this Sat at 3:15pm-4:15pm
Taxes to accountant?	April 5, 2016
Change lightbulbs on front porch	April 5, 2016
Put the kickstand on Jr.'s bike	April 10, 2016
Research car insurance (Are we paying too much? Any deals?)	June 15, 2016
Make reservations for anniversary trip	October 9, 2016
Download 2 boxes of CDs in storage to back up drive	May 1, 2017
Put the Easter decorations in attic!	DANGER! NAG ALERT! (March 28, 2016)

Mother's Day is May 8. :)

Acknowledgements:

First and foremost, I would like to thank the various caregivers who watched my children while I wrote this book. My wonderful mom, Lois Augustine, as well as Erin Park and Colette Shadix handled the bulk of it and for this, I will always be thankful.

I would like to thank my friends and colleagues who gave me their opinions, editing ideas and kind candor while supporting and encouraging me along the way: Ann DuPre Rogers, Mika McAfee, Diane Dexter, Becca Clegg, Veronica Pomeranz, Amy Lewis Bear, Paul Olander, Bernette Sherman, Moshe Mannheim, David Woodsfellow, Casey Truffo, Kelley Colihan, and Tom Johnson.

Many thanks to my Senior Editor-In-Chief and husband, Andrew Flake, who not only helped invent, implement and hone the original Love List, but without whom I never would have known what Joey truly thinks.

I would like to thank my clients who I am blessed to have as my teachers and who have helped the Love List grow and work in wondrous ways that I never would have imagined.

I would like to thank my family who loves me and supports me always.

I would like to thank God who gives me everything and shows me how to help people love themselves as He has loved me.

Made in the USA
Middletown, DE
29 October 2016